D1117401

ADAPTED TO SURVIVE

Angela Royston

Chicago, Illinois

an imprint of Capstone Global Library, LLC
Chicago, Illinois

To contact Capstone Global Library please phone 800-747-4992, or visit our website www.capstonepub.com

Edited by Dan Nunn, Rebecca Rissman, and Helen Cox Cannons
Designed by Jo Hinton-Malivoire
Original illustrations © Capstone Global Library Ltd
Picture research by Mica Brancic
Production by Helen McCreath
Originated by Capstone Global Library Ltd
Printed and bound in China

17 16 15 14 13
10 9 8 7 6 5 4 3 2 1

Library of Congress Cataloging-in-Publication Data
Royston, Angela, 1945- author.
Animals that hunt / Angela Royston.
pages cm.—(Adapted to survive)
Includes bibliographical references and index.
ISBN 978-1-4109-6151-8 (hb)—ISBN 978-1-4109-6158-7 (pb) 1. Predatory animals—Juvenile literature. 2. Animals—Food—Juvenile literature. 3. Animals—Adaptation—Juvenile literature. I. Title.

QL758.R69 2014
591.5′3—dc23 2013017641

Acknowledgments
The author and publisher are grateful to the following for permission to reproduce copyright material: Corbis p. 19 (National Geographic Society/© Ralph Lee Hopkins); Getty Images p. 7 (National Geographic/Jim and Jamie Dutcher); Naturepl.com pp. 4 (© Mary McDonald), 10 (© Anup Shah), 12 (© Andy Rouse), 13 (© Steven Kazlowski), 15, 24, 29 bottom right (© Pete Oxford), 16 (© Edwin Giesbers), 18 (© Brandon Cole), 21, 29 bottom left (© Eric Baccega), 23 (© Alex Hyde), 25 (© Sue Daly), 26, 27 (© Ingo Arndt); Shutterstock pp. 29 top left (© Volodymyr Burdiak), 29 top right (© Critterbiz); SuperStock pp. 5 (Biosphoto), 6 (Universal Images Group), 8 (imagebroker.net), 9 (age fotostock), 11, 14 (Minden Pictures), 17 (Angelo Cavalli), 20 (Juniors), 22 (age fotostock).

Cover photograph of a mountain lion (*Felis concolor*) captive in winter habitat reproduced with permission of Getty Images (All Canada Photos/Don Johnston).

We would like to thank Michael Bright for his invaluable help in the preparation of this book.

Some words are shown in bold, **like this**. You can find out what they mean by looking in the glossary.

CONTENTS

GOOD AT HUNTING

Hunters are animals that attack and kill other animals for food. They are called **predators**, and they include large animals, such as tigers, and small animals, such as spiders. Predators are found almost everywhere—wherever there are animals to feed on!

Predators can live in forests, deserts, grasslands, or oceans. These Cape foxes are predators.

WHY DO ANIMALS HUNT?

Living things need food to give them energy. Plants make their own sugary food using the energy of sunlight. Animals cannot make their own food. Many animals, such as deer and mice, eat plants. However, some animals, such as cougars, have to eat meat.

These deer only eat grass and other plants.

Predators hunt other animals in order to **survive**.

DEADLY WEAPONS

Adaptations are special things about an animal's body that help it **survive**. For example, **predators** have deadly weapons, such as sharp claws or **venomous** stings. Hunters also have particular skills that help them find **prey**. They may be particularly good at seeing, smelling, or hearing.

Super Hearing

A wolf can hear sounds up to 10 miles (16 kilometers) away!

LIONS

Lions are hunters, like all big cats. They move fast and have sharp teeth, which they use to kill **prey**. Lions hunt antelope and other plant-eating animals. They creep close to their prey and wait for the right moment to attack.

DID YOU KNOW?
Female lions hunt down prey, but they let the male lion eat first!

POLAR BEARS

Polar bears hunt for seals on the icy Arctic Ocean. The bears have sharp claws and teeth. They often wait by a hole in the ice for a seal to appear, and then they pounce!

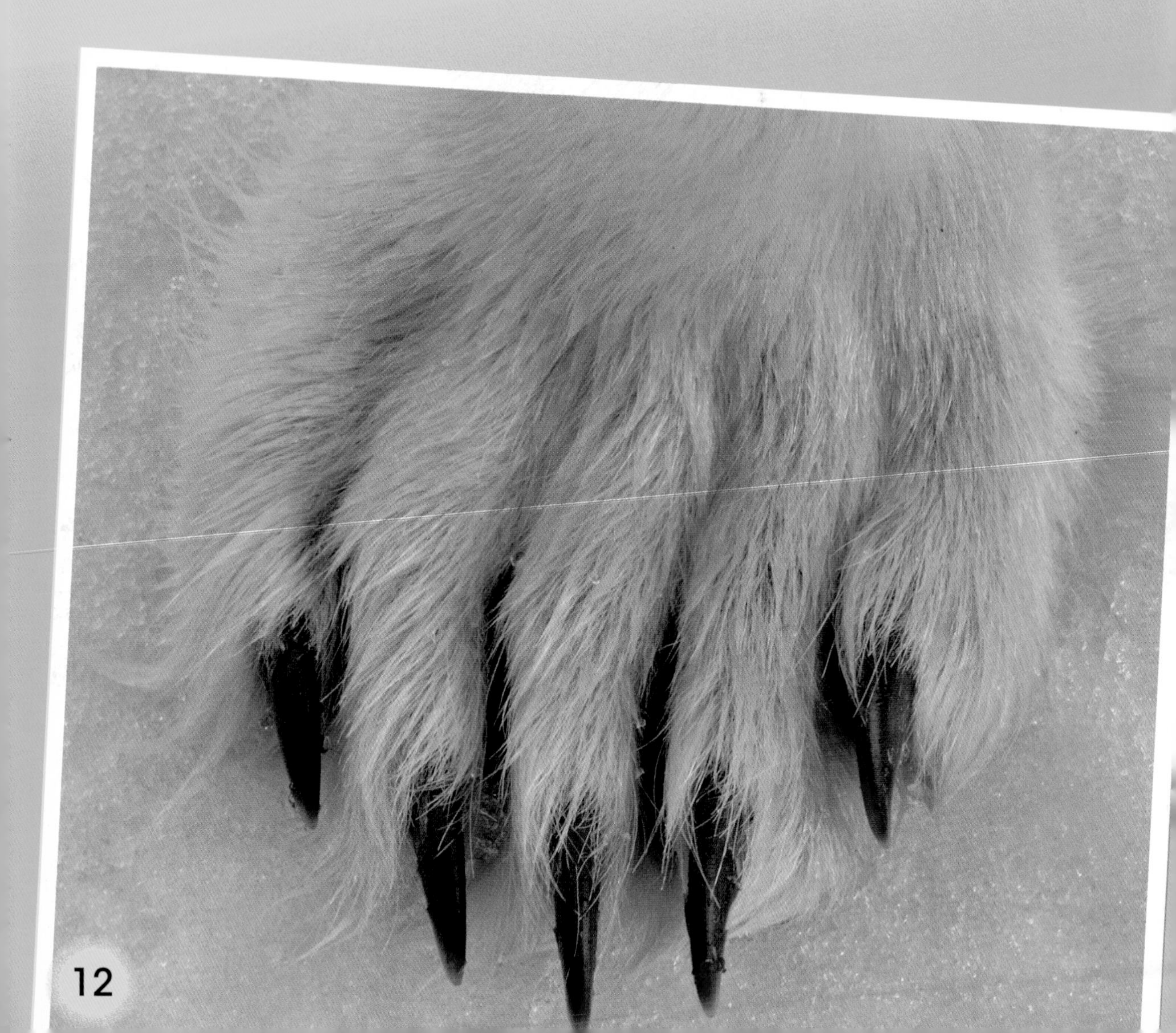

Largest Predator

When an adult polar bear stands on its back legs to attack, it can be more than 10 feet (3 meters) tall!

SHARKS

Sharks have many **adaptations** for hunting. They swim fast. They also have strong jaws and sharp teeth, which rip or crush their **prey**. Sharks have special senses that help them find prey. They can even **detect** tiny movements in the water made by other animals.

DID YOU KNOW?
Sharks can smell the blood of an injured animal 1,640 feet (500 meters) away!

CROCODILES

Crocodiles are **reptiles** that live in rivers, lakes, and ponds. They are well **adapted** to hunting. They have powerful jaws and many sharp teeth. Each tooth has a new tooth growing inside it, ready to take over when the old tooth falls out.

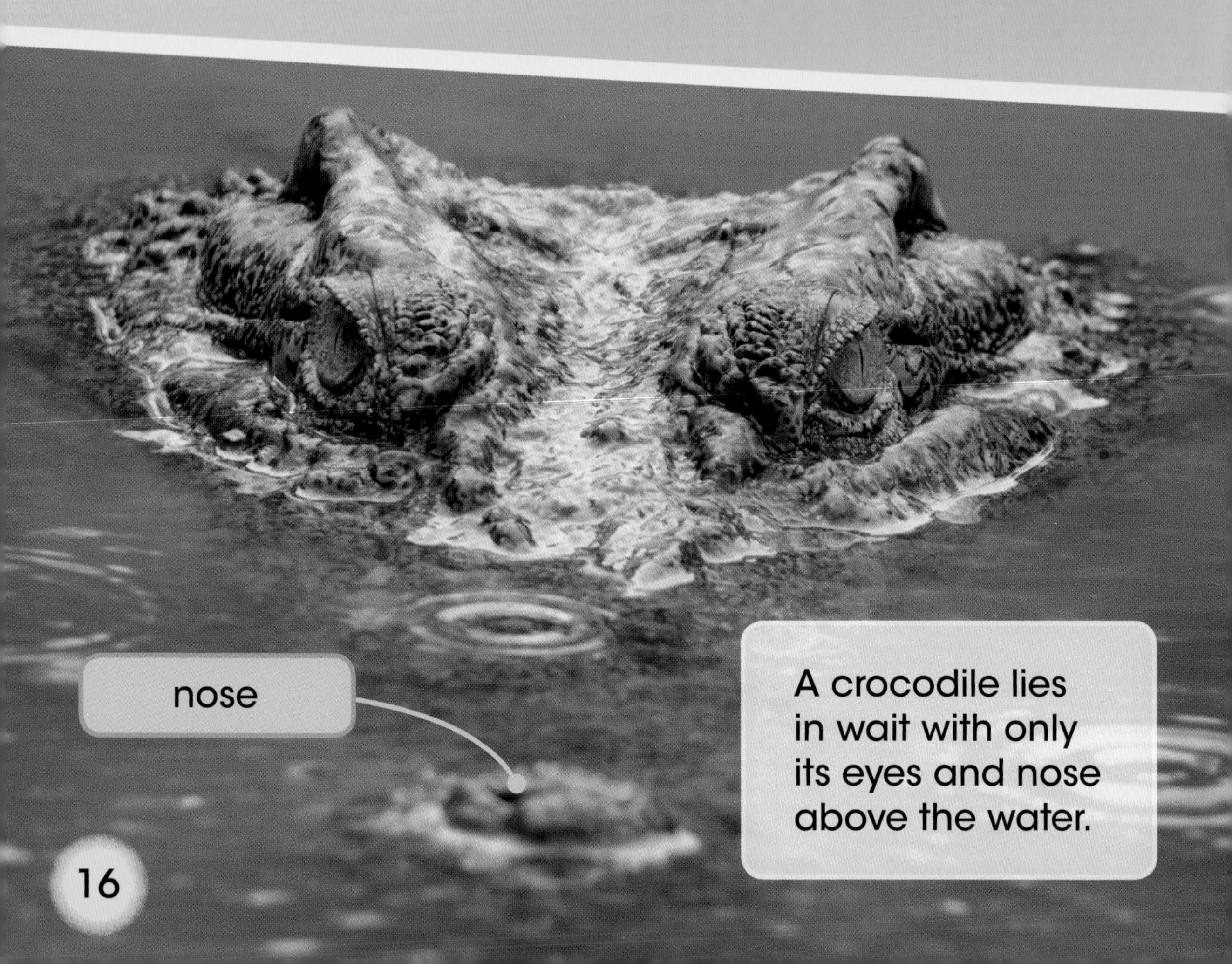

A crocodile lies in wait with only its eyes and nose above the water.

DID YOU KNOW?
A crocodile may go through 3,000 teeth during its life!

KILLER WHALES

Killer whales are the fiercest ocean hunters. A killer whale's **streamlined** body cuts through water, and its sharp teeth tear fish, squid, and other small **prey** before swallowing them whole. Killer whales sometimes hunt alone, but more often they gang up to attack much larger animals.

Groups of killer whales attack sharks and even large whales.

BIRDS OF PREY

Owls and other **birds of prey** grab their **prey** with their two strong legs and sharp claws, called talons. Birds of prey can spot a tiny mouse on the ground far below them. Their hooked beaks tear the meat apart.

Fantastic Eyesight

Birds of prey can see 8 to 10 times better than humans can!

LONG TONGUES

Chameleons and frogs have an amazing **adaptation** for catching food. When an insect flies close, the chameleon or frog whips out its tongue and grabs it! A chameleon's tongue is longer than its body (not counting its tail).

Longest Tongue

A chameleon's tongue can catch an insect up to 5½ inches (14 centimeters) away!

DEADLY POISONS

Many hunters use **venom** to kill **prey**. They include some snakes, spiders, and jellyfish. Snakes and spiders **inject** their venom through hollow fangs. Some box jellyfish are so **venomous** that they can kill a person in less than 5 minutes.

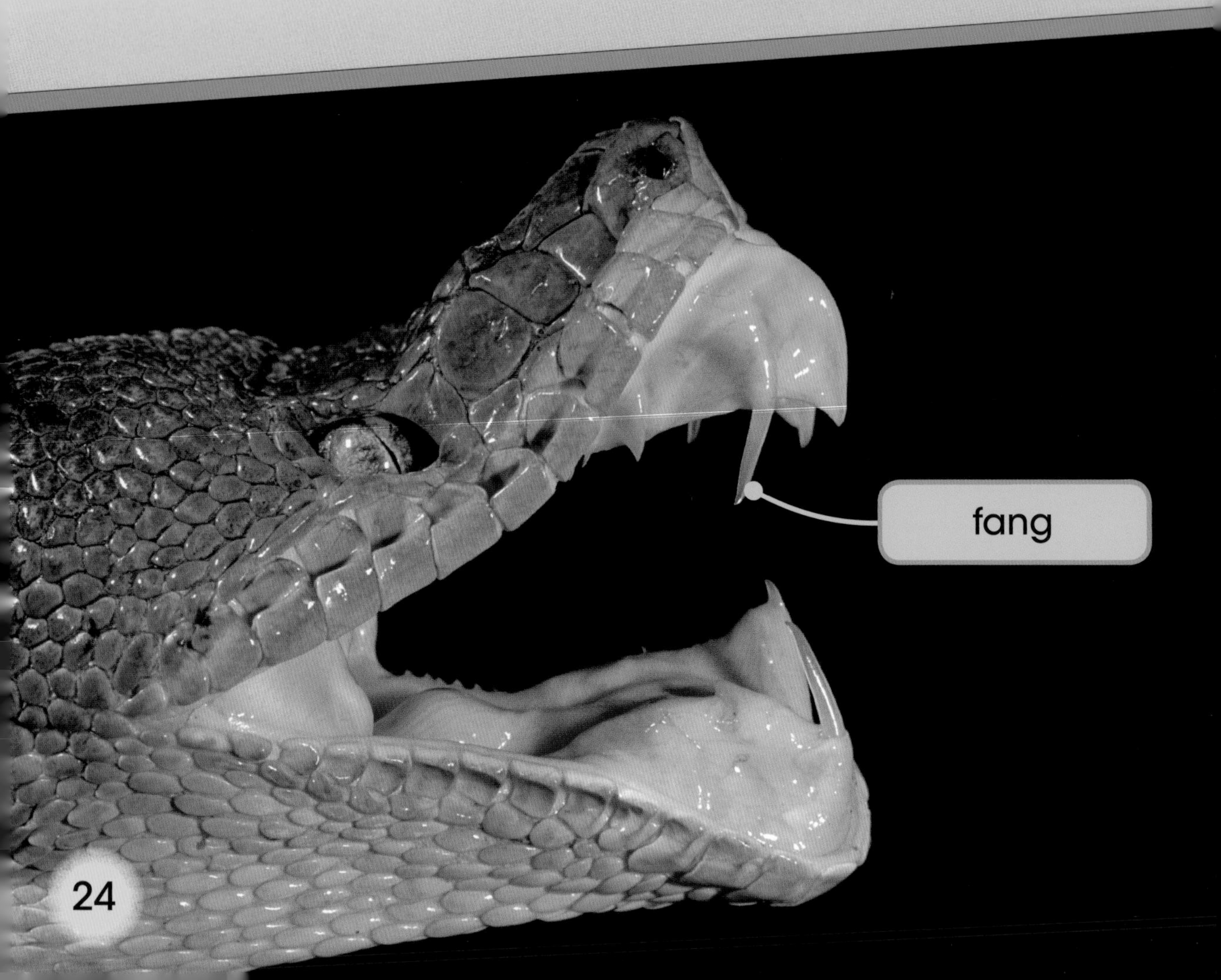

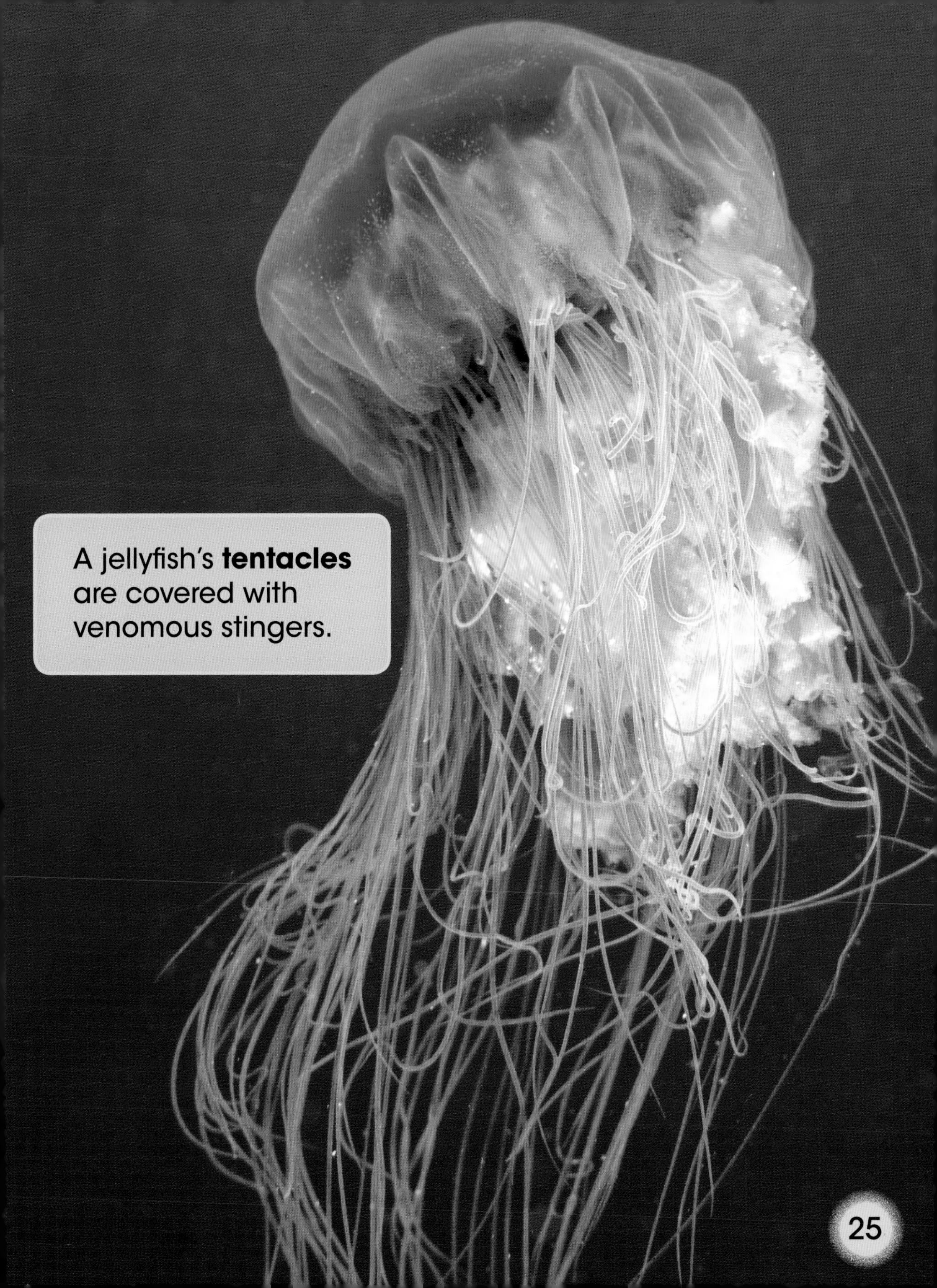

A jellyfish's **tentacles** are covered with venomous stingers.

TRAPDOOR SPIDER

Spiders use **venom** to **paralyze** or kill their **prey**. To catch prey, a trapdoor spider digs a hole and spins a web to cover the opening. The spider hides in the hole and waits. When an insect touches the web, the spider pushes up the trapdoor, leaps out, and catches it.

trapdoor

ANIMAL CHALLENGE

1. Why would an elephant not make a good hunter?

2. What weapons did Tyrannosaurus rex have?

3. What **adaptations** do wolves have for hunting?

Invent your own hunting animal. Think about what animals it might feed on and what weapons it would need. You can use some of the adaptations in the photos, or make up your own.

Answers to Animal Challenge

1. Elephants have tusks and are massively heavy. But they are too big to sneak up on other animals!
2. Tyrannosaurus rex had sharp teeth and strong jaws.
3. As well as good hearing, wolves have sharp teeth. They often hunt in groups, called packs.

GLOSSARY

adaptation special thing about an animal's body that helps it survive in a particular way or in a particular place

adapted well suited to a particular activity or way of living

bird of prey bird that hunts and eats small animals, such as mice and other birds

detect discover or notice

inject force a liquid into the body

paralyze make something unable to move

predator animal that hunts and kills other animals for food

prey animal that is hunted and eaten by another animal

reptile animal that is covered with scales and lays eggs

streamlined smooth, pointed shape that moves through air or water easily

survive manage to go on living

tentacles long feelers that some sea animals use to move and to attack other animals

venom liquid poison that is injected into prey

venomous poisonous

FIND OUT MORE

BOOKS

Ganeri, Anita. *Poison Dart Frog.* Chicago: Heinemann, 2011.

Kolpin, Molly. *Trapdoor Spiders.* Mankato, Minn.: Capstone, 2011.

Rake, Jody Sullivan. *Polar Bears: On the Hunt.* Mankato, Minn: Capstone, 2010.

Riehecky, Janet. *Poisons and Venom (Animal Weapons and Defenses).* Mankato, Minn.: Capstone, 2012.

WEB SITES

FactHound offers a safe, fun way to find Internet sites related to this book. All of the sites on FactHound have been researched by our staff.

Here's all you do:
Visit www.facthound.com
Type in this code: 9781410961518

INDEX